MW01281783

WILD LIFE IN WOODS AND FIELDS

"Eyes and No Eyes" Series

by Arabella B. Buckley

by R. Cadwallader Smith

"EYES AND NO EYES" SERIES   BOOK I

WILD LIFE IN WOODS AND FIELDS

BY

ARABELLA B. BUCKLEY

YESTERDAY'S CLASSICS

CHAPEL HILL, NORTH CAROLINA

Cover and arrangement © 2008 Yesterday's Classics, LLC.

This edition, first published in 2008 by Yesterday's Classics, an imprint of Yesterday's Classics, LLC, is an unabridged republication of the text originally published by Cassell and Company, Ltd. in 1901. For the complete listing of the books that are published by Yesterday's Classics, please visit www.yesterdaysclassics.com. Yesterday's Classics is the publishing arm of the Baldwin Online Children's Literature Project which presents the complete text of hundreds of classic books for children at www.mainlesson.com.

ISBN-10: 1-59915-271-1

ISBN-13: 978-1-59915-271-4

Yesterday's Classics, LLC
PO Box 3418
Chapel Hill, NC 27515

CONTENTS

INTRODUCTION

WE three friends, Peter, Peggy and Paul, walk to school together every day. We all love flowers and animals, and each day we try to find something new.

Peter is a little boy. He can only just read. But he has sharp eyes. He sees most things in the hedges. Peggy's father is a gamekeeper. She knows the birds and where to find their nests. Paul comes from the farm. He is a big boy and will soon be a teacher.

We meet at the big pond under the elm trees. Then we walk along a narrow lane, across the common, through the wood, and over three fields to the village school.

In the pond we find all kinds of creatures. In the lane are beetles and mice, flowers and berries, birds' nests and wasps' nests. On the common the spiders spin their webs on the yellow gorse. In the ploughed field the lark hides her nest. In the grass field there are buttercups and daisies. In the cornfield there are poppies and cornflowers.

Paul is going to write down for us all we see and put it in a book.

CHAPTER I

SPIDERS ON THE COMMON

WHEN we cross the common on a fine summer morning we see many spiders' webs sparkling in the sun. The webs on the gorse bushes are round. They are fastened to the gorse prickles by long silk threads, and each web has spokes like a wheel. These spokes are joined together with rings of silk. There are drops of gum all over the rings. It is these drops which sparkle like diamonds, and make the web so pretty.

The spider spins a little tent in the centre of the web. In this tent she hides, till some insect flies against the gummy threads. Then she feels the web shake, and darts out to catch the fly before it breaks the threads.

We saw a little bee to-day fly right against the web on the gorse bush. Out came the spider from her tent. She bit the bee with her sharp fangs, tore off its wings, and then sat and sucked the juice out of its body.

Paul caught her, while she was busy, and showed us the two fangs with sharp points, which hang down in front of her head. Above them are her eight eyes, four large ones and four small ones. She has eight legs with

2

such strange claws! Each one is like a comb. What do you think they are for? She uses them to guide the silk threads as she makes her web.

We turned her on her back and saw, under her body, six little pockets, out of which she pulls the silk. It comes out through tiny holes. She draws it through the combs on her legs, and so makes her web as she runs along.

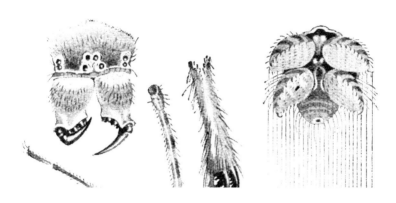

HEAD, LEG, CLAW AND SPINNERETS OF A SPIDER, MUCH MAGNIFIED

Besides the webs on the gorse, there are webs all over the common close to the ground. These are not made with spokes like the round webs. The threads are mixed up like wool. For a long time we could not find the spider. At last one day Paul said, "Here is a hole right in the middle of the web. It goes down into the ground."

A GARDEN SPIDER AND BLACKBERRY BRANCH

This hole was lined with silk threads. Just then a beetle crawled on the web, and shook it. At once the spider darted out from the tunnel in the ground and seized the beetle. She was so quick that she had carried him down into her hole before we could catch her.

There are many spiders on the common which do not spin webs, though they hang from a thread. They spring on the flies and beetles on the ground and are called "hunting-spiders."

The mother hunting-spiders carry their eggs about with them in a round bag. Peter caught one of these as she was running along with this white ball under her body. He took the ball away and put it on the ground. When he let her go, she ran up and seized it. He took

HUNTING SPIDER WITH HER EGG-BAG

it away three times. Each time she caught it up again, and at last ran away before we could catch her.

CHAPTER II

THE WOODPECKER'S NEST

WE were lying under the shade of the trees in the wood one afternoon. All was very quiet, when suddenly we heard such a strange cry. It was like someone laughing, "Yaffil, Yaffil, Yaffil." "That is the woodpecker," said Peggy. "Wait and see what he will do."

So we lay quite still under the tree. Soon the sound came nearer, and a great heavy bird, bigger than a large thrush, flew towards us. He was a beautiful bird. His wings were green, and so was his breast. He had yellow on his tail. His head was red, and he had a red streak on his throat. His beak was long and grey.

He came quite close to us, hopping along. Then he stopped, and a long shining tongue came out of his mouth, and went back so quickly that we could scarcely see it.

"He is eating ants," said Peggy. "The tip of his tongue is sticky and he draws them into his mouth."

Then he began to climb the tree so funnily. His tail is quite stiff and wiry, and he bent it against the tree,

WOODPECKERS

OLD COCK BIRD, BELOW
YOUNG FULLY-FLEDGED BIRD, ABOVE

and pushed himself up, jump, jump, holding on with his sharp hooked toes. He jumped first to the right, then to the left. Then he ran round the tree and came out on the other side.

All the while he was trying the bark with his beak. Tap, tap, tap. At last he found a soft spot. Then he tore off the bark and ate the grubs, which had made the tree rotten in that place. After this he came down the tree again.

It was so funny to see him. He came down backwards tail first, using it to steady himself. Then he spread his wings and flew slowly away.

A WOODPECKER'S NEST

We crept after him, and by-and-by he stopped at an old elm tree and flew round it. Then we could see no more of him.

"His nest must be in this tree," said Peter. "Give me a back, Paul, and I will soon find it."

So Paul let Peter climb on his back till he could

reach the branches of the tree. Then Peter caught hold of the boughs, and crept round the trunk.

"Here it is," he cried at last. "There is a small hole, just big enough for a bird to creep in. But they have made such a big hole inside the tree. I can only just reach down."

Then Peter drew his hand back with the mother bird in it. Her head was not so red as the father's, and she had no red whiskers. He let her fly away and then pulled out six white shining eggs.

"I can feel a number of soft chips of wood at the bottom of the hole," said he. "Shall I put the eggs back?"

"Of course," said Paul; "then the mother will fly back and sit on them, and we will come again and see the little birds when they are hatched."

So we went away. But every day, as we came from school, we turned aside to see if the little woodpeckers had come out of their shells.

At last one day we saw the old woodpeckers carrying insects into the hole. After some time we saw the young birds out on the tree. They could not fly. But they ran about the branches, and jumped so funnily with their stiff tails.

A week later we saw them flying about, and when we came again they were all gone. Peter climbed up and found the nest quite empty.

CHAPTER III

SPRING FLOWERS

WE are always glad when April comes. Then we can find many flowers on our way to school. Even in February there are snowdrops in the orchard and Peter knows where he can sometimes find a primrose or violet in flower.

But we cannot get a good bunch until April. Before that the plants are busy growing their leaves.

The first bright flowers we find are the daffodils in the fields, and the anemones in the woods. We call the daffodils "Lent lilies" and we put them in

DAFFODILS AND ANEMONES

the church at Easter. They have very long, narrow leaves which come straight out of the ground. Each flower hangs on its own tall stalk. It has a deep yellow tube in the middle, with a crown of pale yellow leaves round it. If you dig up a daffodil plant you will find that it has a bulb like an onion. Paul says this is why it blooms so early. It stores up food in the bulb in the autumn. Then it uses this food in January to make its leaves and flowers.

The wood-anemone is Peggy's favourite flower. It is called the "wind-flower" because it nods so prettily in the wind. Its soft pink and white flower stands high up on a long stalk, which has three feathery green leaves half-way down. When the sun shines, it is a little pink and white cup, and when the clouds gather and the rain falls, it shuts up in a tight bud, till sunshine comes again.

Peggy once bit one of the leaves of the anemone. It burnt her tongue and tasted very bitter. Then Paul told us that the plant is poisonous. This is one reason why there are so many anemones in the wood. Animals will not eat the leaves, but leave them alone to grow.

The anemone has not got a bulb. It has a thick brown stem under the ground in which it stores its food.

Before the daffodils and anemones are over, the primroses and violets cover the banks. It is pretty to watch the primrose plant on a wet morning. The leaves are not smooth. They have hills and valleys all along them. The water runs so cleverly down the valleys of the leaf. These guide it down to the roots, so that the plants can drink.

How busy, too, the bees and flies are. They settle first on one primrose then on another. We know what they find there. If you pull off the yellow crown of the primrose, and suck the end of the tube, you will taste something sweet. This is the honey that the bees come to find. And besides the honey they carry off some yellow dust from flower to flower. Paul says this is good for the flowers, as we shall learn some day.

The honey in the violets is not so easy to find. But we have found it. When a violet looks straight at you, it shows five purple leaves and a little yellow beak in the middle. But if you look behind, you will find a small long bag, like the finger of a glove. We have often pulled this off and sucked it. It is full of honey. When the bee sits on the flower, and thrusts her head into the yellow beak in the middle, she sips out the honey with her tongue from the bag or spur behind the flower.

With primroses and violets and blue-bells the bees can now find plenty of honey to fill their hives.

CHAPTER IV

A FAMILY OF SQUIRRELS

WE have a pet called Bobby, and we love him very much. He is a little squirrel, living among the beech trees of the wood.

We see him every morning leaping from branch to branch, with his long furry tail stretched out behind. Sometimes he leaps right down on to the ground and runs about picking up beech nuts.

Sometimes he sits bolt upright on a branch, with a nut or acorn in his paws. Then his tail is bent up against his back.

We have known him for two years, and when we whistle to him he comes to us. But if anything frightens him he darts away to the nearest tree. He climbs up in a moment with his sharp claws, and peeps back through the green leaves. We see his bright black eyes looking down at us.

His back is covered with a brown red fur, but under his body the fur is white. His lovely red tail is like a brush on his back. His hind legs are long. That

13

is why he can jump so well. On his front paws one toe stands out from the others, almost like our thumb. He uses his paws like hands, when he sits up with a nut in them, and peels off the brown skin with his teeth.

Sometimes he steals birds' eggs. Then he holds the egg in his paws, cracks the top, and sucks out the yolk.

He has such funny ears! They have long tufts of hair behind them. He sometimes comes out of his hole in winter to eat, and we see that the tufts are much longer then than in summer.

But for most of the winter we never see him. He is fast asleep in a hole in a tree. We know where his hole is, for Peter found it once. He had seen Bobby come down one mild day to feed on his store of acorns, buried at the foot of the tree, and he watched him as he went back. Then he climbed up the tree, and in a hole in the trunk he saw Bobby's bushy tail curled round. So he knew that Bobby was snug and cosy in the hole.

Bobby has a little wife, and they always keep near each other. But she is very shy, and will not come to us. In the spring, when there are no nuts, they eat the buds of the trees.

About May they are very busy. They gather leaves, and moss, and twigs. These they weave into a nest in the fork of the tree, far from the ground. Then in June their little ones are born. Paul climbed up and saw four such

A PAIR OF SQUIRRELS

lovely little squirrels, covered with soft red and white fur. They stayed in the nest for some time, though we often saw them moving about among the branches. The old squirrels took such care of them, and they stayed together all the summer. In the autumn they hid little heaps of nuts and acorns at the foot of the tree, to eat when they should awake in the mild days in winter.

Then we did not see them again. We do not know whether they all crept into one hole, or whether they each found a hole, and curled themselves up to sleep.

CHAPTER V

THE SKYLARK AND HER ENEMY

THERE are a great many larks near our home. They sing so gaily in the morning as we go to school. But they sing much earlier than that.

We wanted once to try if we could get up before the lark. So we agreed to meet at five o'clock in the morning, in the meadow where one has been singing all this year. We heard him before we got out of the lane. There he was, rising up into the air, going a little to the right, and then a little to the left, rising and singing all the time, as if he wanted to wake all the world with joy.

We watched him till he was quite a tiny speck in the sky. Then he came down again. When he was only a few feet from the ground he shut his wings and dropped into the grass.

The next morning we went at four o'clock. That lark was not singing, but one in the next field was rising up as gay as a lark could be. Then our mothers said we must not get up any earlier. So we could not rise before the larks.

We caught a lark once to look at it, and then let it fly away again. It is not a gay bird. It has brown wings marked with dark streaks. Its breast and throat are a dull white, dotted with brown spots, and it has a white streak

above its eye. Its feet are curious. The toes lie flat on the ground, and the hind toe has a very long claw. If you watch a lark you will see that he runs, he does not hop. Neither does he perch in the trees, and only some-times on a low bush. He lives on the ground, except when he rises up to sing.

THE LARK SOARING

In the winter, as we go to school, we see large flocks of larks in the fields, looking for insects, and seeds of wheat and oats. When we come near them, they get up, a few at a time, and fly away a little further. Then they wheel round and settle down to feed.

In the winter they scarcely ever sing. It is in the spring, when they pair, that they sing so beautifully.

About March we can often find a lark's nest hidden in the grass. They build in a rut, or a little hollow

A LARK ESCAPING FROM A HAWK

in the ground, often in the middle of the field. They line the nest with dry grass, and lay four or five eggs in it. The eggs are a dirty grey colour with brown spots on them, and they lie very snugly in the thick tufts of grass.

When the lark comes down after singing he does not drop close to the nest but a little way off. Then he runs up to the nest through the grass. This is because he is afraid that the sparrow-hawk might see the nest, and pounce on the little ones.

The sparrow-hawk is the lark's great enemy. One day we were looking at a lark rising up, and all at once we saw a sparrow-hawk just going to pounce upon it. The lark saw him too, and darted up faster than the hawk could soar. Then the hawk flew away a little and hovered about till the lark was tired and was obliged to come down. Then once more the hawk tried to pounce. But the lark was too clever for him. He closed his wings and dropped right down into the thick grass, and the hawk could not find him. We were glad the little lark was safe, and got back to his wife and little ones.

CHAPTER VI

NUTS AND NUT-EATERS

WE pass through a small nut-wood on our way to school. In the winter, when there are no leaves on the trees, we see the grey clusters which we call "lambs-tails" hanging on the nut-bushes, Paul says their real name is "catkins."

We often look at them to see how they grow. At first they are only like little grey buds on the branch. Then they grow larger and hang down. By degrees they become very loose, like tassels, and under the grey scales come some little bags of yellow dust.

Then in March, still before the leaves are on the trees, the wind shakes the tree and blows the yellow dust about.

By this time we find small flowers, growing near the end of the branches. You have to look well to find them. But they are very pretty. Each flower has two tiny red horns, and there are many flowers in one green cup.

We know that these red flowers grow into nuts,

THREE KINDS OF WILD NUTS, RED-TIPPED,
NUT-FLOWERS AND CATKINS ON A BRANCH

for we find the nuts just in that place in September. When the wind blows the yellow dust out of the lambs-tails, some of it falls on the red horns of the flowers, and this makes the nut grow.

In the autumn we look out well to see when the nuts are ripe. We want to get some before the Squirrels, and the little birds called Nuthatches, carry them all away.

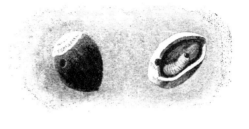

MAGGOTY NUTS

Peggy is in such a hurry that she picks them sometimes before they are ripe. This is foolish, for then there is only a very small watery kernel inside. The rest of the shell is filled with white soft stuff.

Paul says this white stuff is the food which the nut uses to make itself large and firm. When the nuts are ripe they drop quite easily out of the brown leafy cup in which they sit.

Sometimes when we pick the nuts we find one with a little hole in the shell. Then we know that the nut is a bad one, and we shall most likely find a maggot inside.

It is so curious! Paul tells us that this maggot is a

young beetle. It does not look like one. But many beetles when they are young have no legs and are only grubs.

This nut-beetle is called a Weevil. When the nut is quite young and soft, the mother weevil comes and lays an egg in it. She is a very small beetle and has a long snout. With her snout she makes a hole in the soft green nutshell, and then lays a tiny egg in the hole. By-and-by the egg hatches into a maggot. It grows fat by feeding on the nut. So when we gather it, the nut is half eaten, and the maggot is curled up inside.

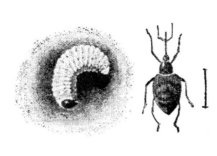

NUT WEEVIL AND GRUB
a. Real Size of Weevil

If we had not picked the nut, the maggot would have eaten a large hole in the nutshell with its horny mouth, and then have crept out of its maggot skin as a little weevil with wings.

So the yellow dust and the red flowers make nuts. Some of these nuts we get. Some the squirrels get. Some the nuthatch gets. Some fall to the ground and grow up into young nut trees, and some the weevil grub gets, before they are ripe.

CHAPTER VII

THE MOUSE AND THE SHREW

PETER has a fine old cat. She is very clever. She rattles the handle of the front door when she wants to come in. If she comes home very late at night she jumps on the wire which runs along the garden wall. This rings a bell, and Peter comes down and lets her in.

But in one thing she is very stupid. She cannot learn that a shrew and a mouse are not the same kind of animal. We are glad when she catches the mice in the garden and in the field. For the mice eat our peas and the bulbs of our crocuses. They hide in the corn-ricks and eat the wheat and oats.

But shrews eat insects and worms and slugs, and this is good for us, because insects and slugs eat our plants.

It is so silly of Pussy, for she ought to know. When she has killed them, she does know them apart, for she eats a mouse and likes it, but she will not eat the shrew. She only kills it and leaves it lying on the path. We think she kills it because it runs away; and does not eat it because it has a bad smell.

HARVEST MICE WITH NEST, ABOVE;
AND FIELD MOUSE BELOW

A great many people do not know a mouse from a shrew, for they are very much alike. A shrew is not quite so large as a field-mouse, and a little larger than the dear little harvest-mouse, which makes a round nest of dry grass among the corn-stalks.

We found one of these nests last summer. It was about as big as a large swan's egg, and the same shape. We peeped inside and found seven wee little harvest-mice, with red-brown fur on their backs and white fur underneath.

The shrew is more of a grey colour. But there is one way by which you can always tell a mouse from a shrew. The mouse has a short snout, and four broad white teeth in front. It uses these for gnawing roots and bulbs, and biting the ears of corn.

But the shrew has a long, thin snout, and its crown teeth are very small and pointed, so that it can kill and eat insects, worms, and snails.

Shrews and mice are both very busy in the evening. We go out sometimes to watch them when the moon is shining. The mice run along so fast out into the field and back to the hedge. Paul says they are carrying seeds and bits of roots into their hole in the bank. For they know that they will want food when they wake up in the winter, and there is none to be found. The shrews move more quietly under the hedge. They push their long snouts into the thick grass, and eat the earwigs and caterpillars.

Both the mice and the shrews are very much afraid of the Barn Owl, which comes out at night and carries them away in her sharp claws to feed her young owls.

Shrews do not store up food, for they sleep in a hole in the bank all the winter through. Then in the spring they line the hole with soft dry grass, and there the mother brings up five or six little shrews.

The mouse, too, burrows deep into the bank. She lays up a nice store of food and goes to sleep. But she often wakes and has a feed, and goes to sleep again. She brings up a great many families in a year. That is why there are so many mice.

BARN OWL AND SHREW

CHAPTER VIII

THE ANT-HILL

THERE is a big ant-hill in the wood on the way to school. It is at the foot of the old oak tree, near the path, and is almost as tall as Peter. It looks like a loose heap of leaves, mixed with sticks and earth. It is broad at the bottom, and round at the top.

HILL OF THE WOOD-ANT

When we come home in the evening all is quiet on the ant-hill. We cannot see even one ant outside. It looks as if no one lived there. But when we pass in the morning, and the sun is warm and bright, we can see the ants creeping out of the cracks and running about the heap.

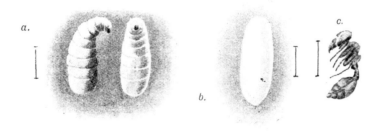

a. AN ANT-GRUB.   *b.* AN ANT-COCOON.   *c.* A YOUNG ANT.
(Much magnified. The lines show the real size.)

They are as big as a grain of barley, and have a tiny knob in the middle of their body. They have long feelers and strong jaws. They bite hard if you touch them. But they do not sting with their tails, as our house ants do.

At dinner-time we find them still more busy. They have opened many holes in the hill, and hurry to and fro. Some fetch bits of leaves and sticks, and add them to the heap. Others bring in food. One day Paul saw a number of ants pulling a dead worm to pieces. Then each ant carried a tiny bit in her jaws to the hill, and went in at a hole.

Sometimes the ants bring some little white lumps in their mouths out of the hill. Peggy's father, the gamekeeper, gives these white lumps to his birds to eat. He calls them ant-eggs. But Paul says they are not eggs. They are baby ants shut up in silk bags, and they are called "cocoons."

Real ant-eggs are much smaller. When the baby ant comes out of the egg it is blind and has no legs. It is called a grub. The nursing ants feed it with honey, and it puts a silk thread out of its mouth and spins a bag round itself.

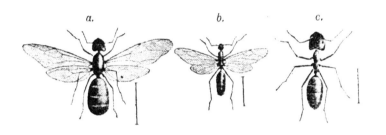

a. MOTHER ANT.   *b.* FATHER ANT.   *c.* WORKER ANT.
(Much magnified. The lines show the real size.)

When the bag is done, the nurses cannot feed the grub any more. So they take care of it. They carry it up to the sunshine by day, and down below at night. Inside the bag, the grub grows into a real ant, with eyes and legs. Then the nurses help it out of its prison, and it begins to work.

One day Paul poked a hole in the ant-hill with

his stick. We saw in the ground, under the leaves, a hollow place full of white cocoons. The ants were very angry. Some bit us, others picked up the cocoons in their jaws and ran away, for fear we should hurt their babies.

When we came back in the evening the ants had mended the hill. Every hole was closed, and all the cocoons were safe inside.

One day in summer we saw a number of ants with wings, flying over the ant-hill. Paul says these are the father and mother ants. The ants without wings are the nurses and workers.

CHAPTER IX

THE HUMBLE BEE'S NEST

LAST March, when the days began to be warm, we saw a big Humble Bee, or Bumble Bee, as the little ones call it, buzzing along across the field.

"Look out, Peter," said Peggy; "that is a mother humble bee, who has been asleep all the winter. She must be making a nest." So Peter followed her. She flew to a bank, and went in among some tufts of grass. Peter put a large stick there and we went to see her every day.

We used to find her dragging in little pieces of moss. But we did not look in, for fear she should go away. After a fortnight Paul said we might look, and, hidden in the grass, we found a small round patch of moss lined with bees-wax. It was like a tiny saucer turned upside down. We lifted it up and found under it a few round flat pockets, some as big as a halfpenny, some not larger than a farthing. They were made of brown, sticky wax, and when we opened one we found inside seven tiny eggs, as small as poppy seeds, and some little brown balls. The balls, Paul said, were made of honey, and of the yellow dust from flowers. In another pocket we found grubs which had already been hatched from eggs. These were feeding on the brown balls near them.

A HUMBLE BEE'S NEST

The mother bee was very uneasy while we were looking at her nest. She sat down quite near. We could see how big and stout she was. She was so handsome. Her brown body was covered with soft yellow hairs, with stripes of black hairs between. Her wings were broad, and shone so brightly in the sun. She did not sting us. Paul says that humble bees are very gentle. But she was afraid we should hurt the grubs, which were going to grow up into working bees. We put the cover back and waited two months. Then it was June. We were

HUMBLE BEES GATHERING HONEY FROM PEA-FLOWERS

afraid the horses might tread on the nest when the hay was cut. So we went to look at it.

Oh! how big it was now. There was a large round moss roof. It was lined with wax, and was so strong that we had to cut it with a knife. The only way for the bees to get into it was by a long tunnel just under the ground. Under the roof were a number of dirty yellow silk cocoons. In these were the grubs, growing into humble bees. The cocoons were stuck together with wax. Some of them were open, for the young bees had come out. These had honey in them.

There were a great many humble bees going in and out. These had all come from eggs laid by the mother bee in two months. They were very busy bringing in honey and bee-bread for the grubs to eat. But Paul says they do not store honey, like our hive-bees. For when the cold damp weather comes, they all die, except a few mothers. These creep into holes in the trees or into a warm haystack, and sleep till the spring comes again.

About Christmas time we went to look at the nest. The roof was broken, and the cells all crushed. There was not one humble bee to be found.

CHAPTER X

PETER'S CAT

PETER's cat is very fond of going into the wood. We are afraid she will be killed some day. For Peggy's father shoots all the cats he finds in the wood, because they eat the rabbits and pheasants.

But Peter cannot keep her at home. As soon as it gets dusk, she slips out, and often does not come home all night. She goes in the dusk, because then all the animals are feeding. So she can catch mice and young rabbits, as well as partridges asleep on the ground, and other birds in the trees.

She is a very clever hunter. Her body is so well made for catching her prey. She is slender, but very strong. She can kill a mouse with one stroke of her paw. She can spring ever so far, and so quickly that few mice or birds can escape her.

Then she has soft pads under her feet, so that she can creep along very quietly. And she can jump down from a high wall because the soft pads keep her feet from being hurt when she reaches the ground.

37

A CAT STALKING A RABBIT

We all know what sharp claws she has at the end of her toes. But when she is playing with her kitten or with Peter, her paw is so soft you would not think she could scratch. This is because she has a groove in each toe under the skin, and when she does not want her claws, she draws each one back into its own sheath.

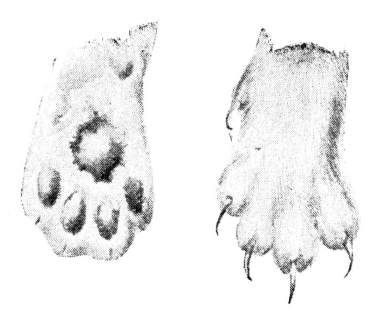

PADS AND CLAWS ON PUSSY'S FEET

But when she springs on a mouse or a bird, she strikes with her paw, and as she bends her toes, out come the claws and pierce the flesh of her prey.

But how does she see the rats and mice in the night? Paul showed us that she can open the middle of her eye very wide in the dark. We took pussy near to the lamp and saw the hole or "pupil" of her eye was only a little narrow slit. Then we shut her up in a dark room for some minutes, and took her outside, and looked at her

eyes in the moonlight. The little slit had become a large round *a* black hole.

The slit lets in enough light for pussy to see in the daytime, and when she goes out at night the slit stretches out into *b* a big round hole which lets in all the light there is, from the moon or the stars.

But if it is very dark indeed, she feels her way with her whiskers. Paul says it is very cruel to cut a cat's whiskers, for they are a great help to her in the dark.

CAT'S EYES.
a. In the light.
b. In the dark.

Pussy has a very rough tongue. If you let her lick your hand, you will feel how different it is from your own tongue, or that of a dog. It is so rough that she can rasp the scraps of meat off a bone, after she has torn away the flesh with her long pointed front teeth.

Pussy is very clever in getting her living, and if you look at her head you will see why. For she has a good broad forehead with plenty of room inside for a large brain. We put a rabbit's head near hers the other day. It was so narrow, and had so little room for a brain we were not surprised that the cat is too cunning for him.

Who would think that Pussy, who sits and purrs with her kitten by the fire, is so fierce in the wood? But Paul says that there were once wild cats in Scotland and in the north of England, and they were as fierce as tigers. Tigers and cats are very much alike. Tigers can be loving too. We heard a tiger purr one day in a wild beast show, when she was licking her cub.

CHAPTER XI

THE GREEDY STRANGER

IT was the middle of April this year when we first heard the cuckoo. We love to hear it, for it tells us that spring has come. This year we were very lucky. We saw a young cuckoo grow up in his nest.

This was how it happened.

We had heard the cuckoo for some time, cuck-oo, cuck-oo, and it seemed as if many cuckoos were singing. One day we heard such a funny noise, like kik-kik-kik. "Ah!" said Peggy, "father says that is the cry of the mother cuckoo which lays the eggs. That is why there are so many cuckoos about. They are singing to her."

"Well then," said Peter, "if she stops here, perhaps we may find one of her eggs. I do so want to see a young cuckoo."

About a week after this Peter found a titlark's[1] nest. It was in a tuft of grass, on the bank near the wood. Two small dull-grey eggs, spotted with brown, were

---

[1] Now called a "Pipit." But country children know it as the Titlark."

lying in the nest. The next day, as we went to school, there were three eggs. The next morning there were four. But as we came back from school that afternoon there were five eggs.

"The titlark cannot have laid two eggs in one day," said Peter. "I wonder if the cuckoo has brought one of her eggs here."

For we know that the cuckoo lays her eggs on the ground, and brings it in her wide beak to the nest of some other bird. We looked every day for a fortnight. The little titlark was so used to our coming, she did not even fly off the nest. She was a pretty little bird, with brown spotted wings and a yellow throat and chin.

At the end of a fortnight two little titlarks came out of their shells, and the next day two more. They opened their beaks for food, and the father titlark flew out to the field, and brought flies and caterpillars to feed them. But the mother still sat on the fifth egg.

Two day later the fifth bird came out. It had a curved beak, and bent toes with short, sharp claws. Its toes were two in front and two at the back. Titlarks have straight beaks and flat toes, three in front and one at the back.

So we knew our young cuckoo by his beak and toes.

We came next day to look. The little titlarks had quills on their wings where the feathers were growing, and their eyes were open. The cuckoo was naked and blind. But he had pushed two of the titlarks out of the nest, and they lay on the bank quite dead.

The cuckoo had grown bigger even in one day, and the old titlarks kept feeding him with insects as he sat with his beak wide open. While we were looking at

A CUCKOO SINGING

him the cuckoo pushed about in the nest and shoved another little titlark over the edge, on to the bank. We put it back in the nest and then we had to go on to school. When we came back the cuckoo sat in the nest alone. All the four little titlarks were dead on the bank. He had pushed them all out.

The old birds did not seem to see their dead children. They were so busy feeding the big hungry stranger. They fed him for five or six weeks, even after he could come out of the nest.

It was so funny to see! The cuckoo was larger than a thrush and the titlarks not bigger than a sparrow. Yet the big bird sat on a branch with his beak open, and let these little birds carry all his food.

At last he flew away. We heard a cuckoo singing in August, when we knew the old birds were all gone. We wondered if it was our young "greedy stranger."

CHAPTER XII

THE MOLE AND HIS HOME

THERE were so many moles in the barn field last summer. We used to see mole heaps thrown up all over the field. At last Paul's father sent for the mole-catcher. He put traps in the runs and brought in many dead moles.

A mole is a curious creature. We country children call him a "wunt." He has a long, plump body, and a short, stumpy tail. His dark brown fur is like velvet, it is so soft and close. He has a long, pointed snout, very hard at the tip, and his mouth is full of strong, sharp teeth.

His feet are very curious. They have no fur on them, but are naked and pink. His front paws are like broad, flat hands with very strong claws. They turn away from his body, and look too big for such a small, soft creature.

Paul says these paws are the mole's shovels. He lives under the ground and catches worms to eat. As he goes along he makes a hole with his hard nose, and then shovels away the earth with his strong hands. In this way he makes a tunnel, and when he wants to get rid of the loose earth, he pokes it above ground with his long snout. This is how the mole-hills are made.

MOLE EATING A WORM

But the moles do not always stay under the ground. We have seen them sometimes on a warm summer's evening poking about in the hedges, looking for slugs and snails. There are more he-moles than she-moles.

We wanted so much to find a mole's home. We dug down below some of the mole-hills hoping to find one. But we only found a tunnel. The mole-catcher laughed at us for digging there. He asked us if we thought that the mole would put a heap of loose earth over his home, to tell his enemies where to find him.

At last, one day a gentleman came to Paul's

father and asked him to open a mole's home for him. He wanted to see what it was like. This was just what we wanted, so we went too.

The mole-catcher took us some way across the field. At the corner near the wood we came to a large mound, under the trees, covered with grass.

Then he began to dig away the side of the mound. By-and-by, about the middle, he stopped and cleared away the earth very carefully with his hands. And there, just below the ground, was a big round hole covered with a roof of very hard earth. He had taken away the side, and we could see in. The hole was lined with dry grass, and in it lay four tiny moles. We filled it in again very carefully and left the baby moles safe and quiet.

We saw four holes in the sides of the nest. These led to the runs through which the old moles went in and out to feed. We are afraid they got rather filled with earth from our digging, but the mole-catcher said that they would soon be put right by the old moles.

He says that the father mole lives in another home like this all alone in winter, feeding on worms. Sometimes he comes up above the ground, and if it is very frosty weather he dies of cold. He only takes a wife in the spring.

CPSIA information can be obtained
at www.ICGtesting.com
Printed in the USA
BVRC091652190721
612141BV00008B/7